CARRICKMACROSS LACE

CARRICKMACROSS LACE

From Beginner to Expert

MOLLIE BUTLER &
ALEXANDRA TRUBSHAW

B T BATSFORD LTD · LONDON

To Friendship

ISBN O 7134 6366 X

Typeset by J&L Composition Ltd,
Filey, North Yorkshire
Printed in Great Britain by
Butler & Tanner Ltd, Frome and London

for the Publisher
B.T. Batsford Ltd,
4 Fitzhardinge Street,
London W 1 H OAH

CONTENTS

ACKNOWLEDGEMENTS

We wish to thank all our friends and the members of our families who have assisted and encouraged us in this venture. We particularly wish to mention Cynthia Pearce for her wonderful and patient help with the typing, and June and Stanley Jackson, who so skilfully photographed our work. We are also indebted to Bob Trubshaw for his indispensable help throughout the project.

INTRODUCTION

It is the aim of this book to introduce Carrickmacross Lace to all who enjoy creating something special. The basic techniques are methodically described. Advanced techniques are also included, as are original patterns suitable for all abilities and many uses. Thus the needs of both the beginner and the more knowledgeable lacemaker are considered.

The making of one piece of lace – a handkerchief corner – is explained in detail so that while learning what to do, and how best to do it, the lacemaker can produce something useful. (There is, of course, no reason why the finished lace could not be used to adorn, for example, a lapel, a cuff or a pocket, if a handkerchief is not required.) The object of the exercise is to produce something worth keeping, and to make learning a pleasure.

The instructions are, of necessity, detailed; it is hoped that the abundance of notes does not obfuscate! The diagrams and photographs which accompany them should, however, make it easier to follow the described procedures. Anyone who has ever wielded a needle and a pair of scissors should have no real problem, providing the advice offered is heeded.

Every opportunity to guide, help and inform, while infusing the lacemaker with enthusiasm and creativity has, it is hoped, been seized upon. Even the section title pages and illustrative motifs have been designed to inspire – first with interest, then with the urge to explore ideas.

The range of patterns encompasses the traditional and the modern. No art form survives unchanged; generations differ, tastes and fashions alter, available materials can either restrict or facilitate. If we can retain what is traditional, yet remain unafraid to experiment, any craft remains alive and exciting. This book is the culmination of that desire.

—1—
ORIGINS

erhaps it was little more than chance that led Ann Steadman to the vicarage. It was probably mere good fortune that enabled her to gain a position in the rector's household. Having secured employment she was not to know how she would be remembered, by whom, and for how long.

Her job was that of a sewing maid and she can be imagined bending over some fabric, stitching with nimble fingers, while her mistress guided and encouraged. Together these two developed a new type of lace, and in doing so created a piece of history. The lace upon which they worked became known as Carrickmacross Lace.

It is not known how much of Ann's time was devoted to lacemaking, nor for how long she laboured. No doubt there were times when her chair or stool would have been drawn closer to the window in order to catch the last rays of the sun as she stitched. Perhaps she was sometimes obliged to work by lamplight, although many daylight hours must have been occupied by Mrs Grey Porter's new interest, for Ann's enterprising mistress made time to instruct other people too. She taught several local women and they may all have gathered to learn how to perfect the recently acquired skill.

There is little factual information about Ann, even her name is uncertain; she is referred to as Ann, Anne or even sometimes Mary. It is believed that she was an accomplished needlewoman and that she lived in Ireland, where she was employed by the Grey Porters of Donaghmoyne in the county of Monaghan. Little more than this is known.

Ann's mistress was the wife of the Reverend John Grey Porter. He was rector of the parish of Donaghmoyne, near Carrickmacross, after which the lace was named. Because of her husband's occupation, and her own standing within the community, it can be assumed that Mrs Grey Porter commanded respect. She was probably able to influence, to a limited extent, popular taste in fashion; she was therefore in a position to foster an interest in the new lace. She must also have had an appreciation of design and skilful needlecraft because it is she who is credited with the introduction of Carrickmacross Lace to Ireland in about 1820.

While on holiday, or perhaps honeymoon, she is reputed to have obtained an example of Italian needlework. She was so impressed by it that on her return home she taught her maid, Ann, to copy it. Ann's work was much admired and several orders were placed. Interest was aroused and gradually spread; people wanted to know more about the lace; some wanted to learn how to make it while others merely desired to own pieces.

This activity attracted the attention of another woman who possessed entrepreneurial skills: Miss Reid of the village of Rahans. She liked the work, acknowledged that her sister would also be interested in it and rapidly realized its potential. It represented a much-needed means of supplementing the meagre income of the poor, should some of them be taught the skill. Together the sisters ran a girls' lace school in a converted outbuilding on their brother's farm. Later Miss Reid established a similar school on her own property. She maintained it until her death, after which control of the school passed to her niece.

In spite of the enthusiasm of both Mrs Grey Porter and Miss Reid, their separate business ventures were not commercial successes. Poor marketing was largely to blame. It was not until hunger and destitution made people desperate, after the famine of 1846, that the lace was viewed as a viable source of income. At about that time a scheme to help the poor increase their earnings was devised by Tristran Kennedy and Captain Morant. The former emulated Miss Reid's attempt to establish lace schools and built several, while the latter founded a central lace school.

The making of the lace was then positively encouraged; the skill rapidly developed and spread to other regions of Ireland. In the 1850s and 1860s it was widely exhibited in Dublin and Cork, on the Continent, in Paris and Milan, in London and even in parts of America. It was not, however, officially known as Carrickmacross until after the Dublin Exhibition in 1872.

The lace was not cheap and, when the designs ceased to keep up with fashion and were marred by sub-standard work, demand understandably declined. The importance of adequate supervision and quality control was underestimated. Neither did the organizers appreciate that good, fashionable design was of considerable importance. Purchasers were not interested in poor-quality lace, and designs that were not in vogue were difficult to sell. By the end of the 1860s the industry was in decline.

Slowly, as the nineteenth century approached its closing decades, interest in Carrickmacross Lace was revived. The revival owed much to the zeal of the nuns at the St Louis Convent at Carrickmacross. They ensured that the skill was not forgotten by teaching the young in the schools. Good designs were obtained and beautiful, elaborate patterns were developed. The prestige of Carrickmacross Lace was restored; the recovering industry gained strength, and the interest it generated was maintained well into the early years of this century.

More than 160 years after its inception the lace is again enjoying a revival. An activity which many today regard as a leisure pursuit was once a means of keeping hunger at bay. Worn or used as decoration, usually by privileged people with adequate incomes, the lace was made by those who often struggled to feed their families. Thus Carrickmacross, which is regarded as one of the oldest of the Irish laces, has its roots deep in the soil of hardship and poverty.

There were two distinctive types of Carrickmacross: the 'appliqué' and the 'guipure'. In the former, motifs outlined with fine cord thread were cut out of muslin or cambric and sewn to a net background. A wide variety of net embroidery stitches was used to embellish the net. Sometimes the motifs were held together with bars of thread over which button-hole stitch was worked. These bars, often referred to as 'brides', produced a 'guipure'. Both techniques were often used in one piece of lace, resulting in a richly ornamented style.

Fluid scrolls, swirling designs, flower and leaf shapes all add to the delight of the lace, but the cutwork, the fillings and 'brides' increase its beauty. At its finest the work is intricate and elaborate, possessing a delicate quality, yet it can also be bold and dramatic.

Interest in this type of lace has grown, as has interest in many other crafts and laces. With increased leisure time, and a genuine desire to keep alive the so easily forgotten skills of past generations, people have demonstrated their eagerness to learn, if only to counteract the stress of modern-day living.

There is, however, something immensely rewarding in creating a thing that is beautiful out of a few pieces of fabric and some thread. To produce Carrickmacross for a living must have been tedious and stressful; to make it now, for pleasure and the satisfaction of achievement, keeps alive not only part of the past, but indulges personal creativity and results in something which would be difficult and, in some cases, impossible to purchase.

Carrickmacross offers tremendous scope for individual artistry. Patterns can be adapted easily, or even designed, providing a few simple guidelines are observed. Fillings can be complex or simple. More, or less, of the fabric can be cut out, depending upon the requirements and skill of the lacemaker. Its production requires a minimum of tools and equipment. Work in progress can be slipped easily into a corner of a bag or briefcase and this may be part of its attraction. Patience is required, as too is good light and a steady hand, but the results and rewards are considerable, even at times, immeasurable.

Mrs Grey Porter and her sewing maid did not waste their time.

—2—

GUIDELINES and MATERIALS REQUIRED

he instructions which follow are intended to help the beginner but may also be of interest to the more experienced lacemaker. By following them carefully a professional finish can be achieved.

It is important to keep the threads clean, to start and finish neatly, and to make tiny, evenly spaced oversewing stitches approximately 1–2 mm ($\frac{1}{32}$–$\frac{1}{16}$ in) apart. These stitches should be worked with the needle pointing towards the centre of the flower, leaf or motif (see FIGURE 9). Important, too, is the lacemaker's ability to cut away unwanted fabric to enhance the design without damaging the needlework, hence the necessity of using a pair of lace scissors.

Carrickmacross Lace is made with organdie and net. The pattern is produced by oversewing a coarse thread with a fine thread, stitching through both layers of fabric. Part of the organdie is cut away, along the outline, to reveal the net beneath. This space can then be filled with net embroidery stitches. Much of the beauty of this lace lies in the fillings, which are dealt with later in the book.

Considerable satisfaction may be gained from producing a simple piece of lace, with comparatively few swirls of pattern, but one which is neatly decorated with buttonhole-stitched circles known as 'pops'. The stitch here referred to as 'buttonhole' is the plain, knot-less variety, sometimes called 'blanket stitch' but known in lace circles as 'buttonhole'.

Materials Required

Pattern or design to be worked

Cotton organdie

Fine cotton net (*not* a square mesh), approximate size: 2.5 cm (1 in) = 20 spaces

Crochet cotton No. 40 (coarse cotton) or any cotton thread of an equivalent thickness

Tanne No. 50 or No. 80
or
DMC Retors d'Alsace No. 50
Any one of these fine cotton threads can be used but it is also possible to use successfully any similar fine cotton thread

Needles: Sharps No. 10 and a Crewel No. 7

Lace scissors

Tracing paper

Marking pen, medium point with blue or black waterproof
ink

FIGURE 1 *Materials
required for working
Carrickmacross lace*

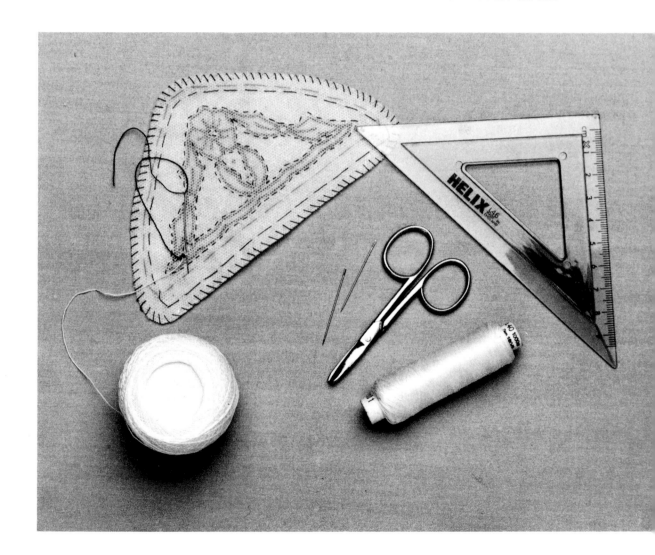

—3—
METHOD

 his handkerchief corner has been specially designed to enable the lacemaker to complete the whole pattern with only one starting and finishing point.

Step 1

(A) With the tracing paper and marking pen, trace the design to be worked (FIGURE 2) leaving a border 2.5 cm (1 in) all round the pattern.

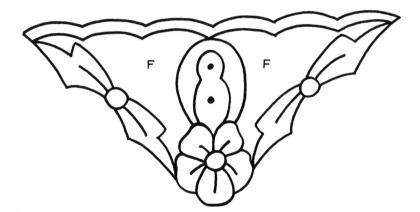

FIGURE 2 *Pattern for the first handkerchief corner*

FIGURE 3 *The handkerchief corner completed, using filling 1 (page 34)*

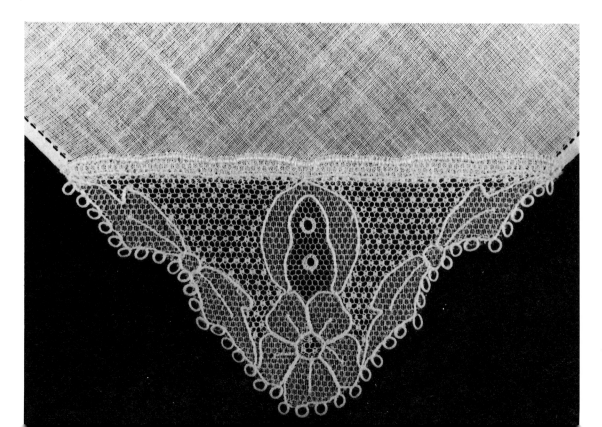

(B) Cut the net to the same size as the tracing paper. Take care that the straight weave of the net is parallel with the top or the base line of the design as in FIGURE 4.

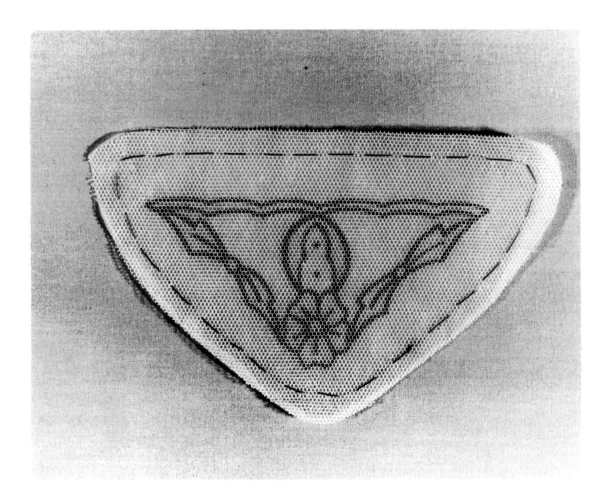

FIGURE 4 *The net is cut to the same size as the tracing paper and then tacked into position*

(C) Put the net on to the reversed side of the traced design as a safeguard against the ink marking the fabric. Tack about 6 mm (¼ in) from the outer edges, keeping the net flat. Ensure that all knots, joins and loose ends are at the back of the work.

(D) Cut the organdie to fit over the net and the tracing paper. Secure this too with tacking stitches about 6 mm (¼ in) from the edges. In FIGURE 5 part of the organdie has been cut away to show the net beneath in an attempt to clarify procedures.

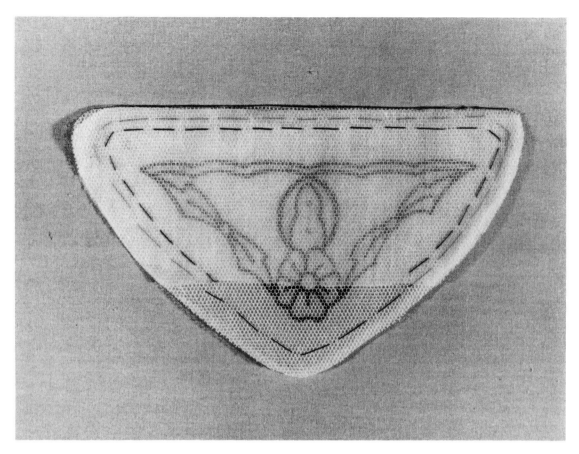

(E) Oversew all three edges to prevent fraying (FIGURE 6).

FIGURE 5 *Tack the organdie into place. Note that part of the organdie has been cut away here to show the net beneath*

FIGURE 6 *Oversewing helps to prevent fraying*

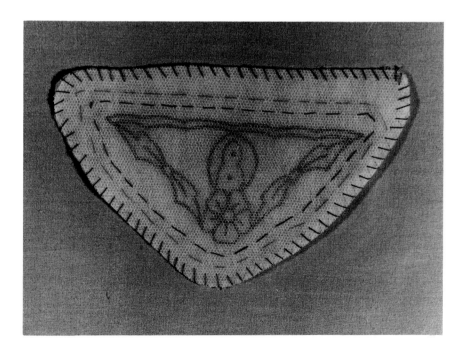

21

FIGURE 7 *Small, neat tacking stitches outline the design*

(F) Next, with stitches approximately 3 mm (⅛ in) long, tack round the outline of the design. It is essential that these stitches do not cross any lines of the design. (FIGURE 7).

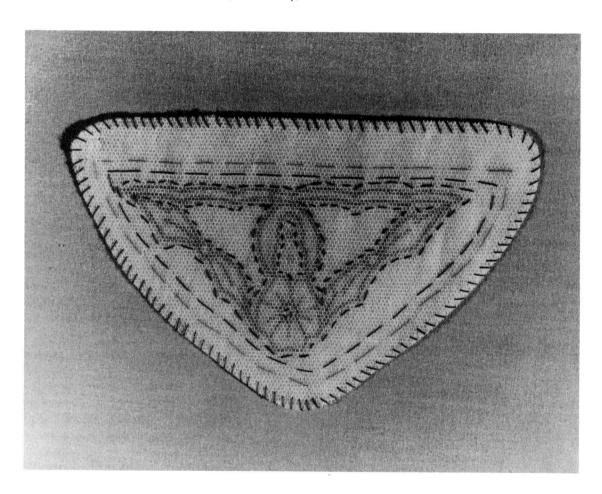

Step 2

(A) Thread a NO 7 Crewel needle with the coarse crochet cotton, No. 40, or a similar thread. Do not cut the thread. Leave it attached to the ball.

(B) At the starting point clearly indicated in FIGURE 8 push the needle from the right side through the organdie, net and tracing paper, to the wrong side of the work. Carefully pull the crochet cotton through all three layers to the wrong side.

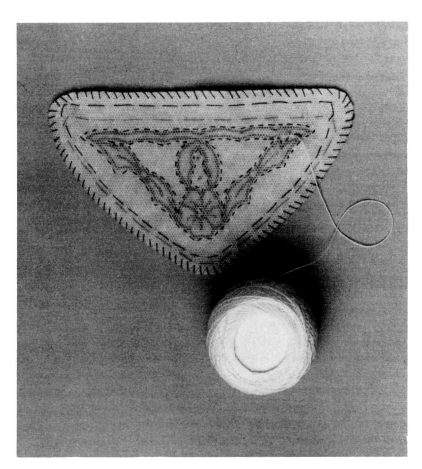

FIGURE 8 *Beginning the work*

(c) Unthread the needle leaving 5 cm (2 in) to be cut off later. A knot tied at the back of the work will help to secure the thread and prevent it from pulling through to the right side when starting work.

(d) Lay the crochet cotton (coarse thread) on top of the organdie along a small section of the design, which should be clearly visible through the net and organdie.

Step 3

(A) Thread a NO 10 (Sharps) needle with fine thread approximately 50 cm (20 in) in length. Remember that if the thread is too long it could tangle, break or become soiled.

(B)   With this fine thread make a small back stitch approximately 2 cm (¾ in) from the starting point, stitching through the organdie and net only. This is followed by three or four running stitches, to secure the fine thread prior to oversewing the coarse thread. Remember to stitch through both the net and organdie but *not* through the tracing paper.

Step 4

(A)   Use the fine thread (which is already secured with a back stitch and running stitches) to make two or three minute, tightly pulled stitches to hold the coarse thread in place at the starting point (FIGURE 9).

FIGURE 9   *A close-up of the handkerchief corner illustrating the importance of pointing the needle towards the centre of the flower, leaf or motif being worked. The black thread represents the fine thread, the white the coarse*

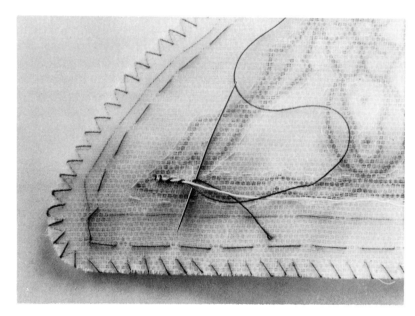

(B)   Following the directional arrows on FIGURE 10, continue oversewing with small, fairly tightly pulled stitches through both the organdie and the net but not through the tracing paper. These stitches should be approximately 1–3 mm (1/16–1/8 in) apart but not touching each other. It is essential to pick up both the organdie and the net when oversewing the coarse thread.

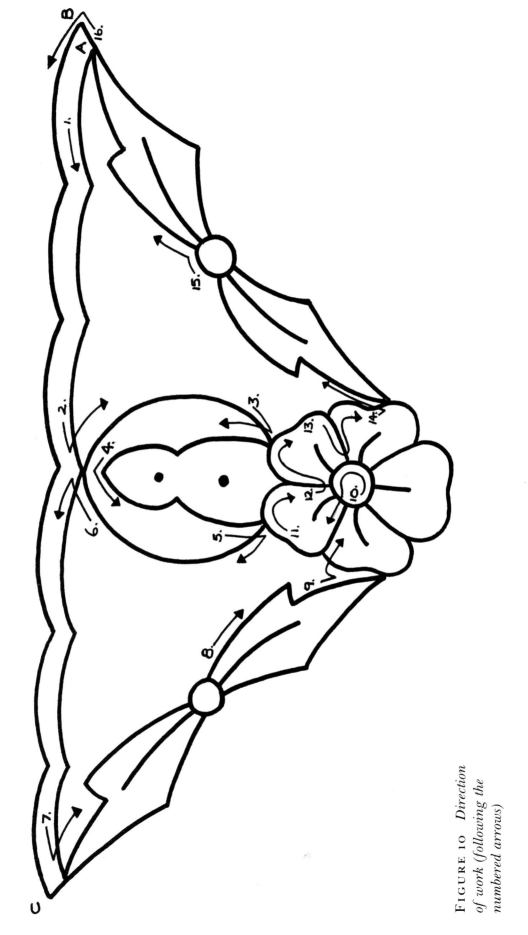

FIGURE 10 *Direction of work (following the numbered arrows)*

Step 5

These following numbered points refer to the numbers on
FIGURE 10.

1 Start at A on the inner edge of the broad top band.
Oversew the coarse thread along the inner line of the top
band following the numbered arrows.

2 Take the thread down the right-hand side of the central
motif.

3 At the point where the coarse thread reaches the top
right petal continue stitching along the line of the central
motif. Make sure that the sharp angles of the design are
retained by securing the points with a well-placed stitch.

4 Stitch round the central motif until the top left petal of
the flower is reached.

5 Continue round the left half of the central motif, towards
the top band.

6 Take the coarse thread along the inner line to the outer
corner of the design.

7 Stitch along the inner edge of the leaf. *Do not cross the
coarse threads.*

8 Continue towards the flower.

FIGURE 11 *The
method of working the
flower in the centre of the
handkerchief corner*

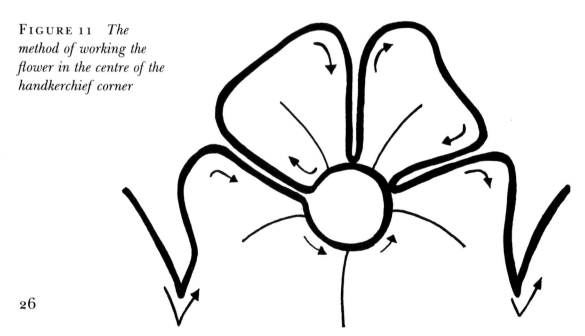

9 At the tip of the leaf lay the coarse thread over the bottom left petal, working towards the centre of the flower. The circle in the centre and the veins are worked at this stage. (FIGURE 11).

10 *Working a vein.* When the first vein is reached take the fine thread up to the tip of the vein where single threads of organdie and net are picked up. Take the fine thread to the base again, securing it with a tiny stitch. Return to the tip of the vein so that three lengths of fine thread lie together along the line of the vein (FIGURES 12 and 13). Oversew these threads, following the line of the vein. Do not pull too tightly as holes may appear in the organdie. All veins are worked in this way. Return to the coarse thread and complete the centre, working each vein in turn.

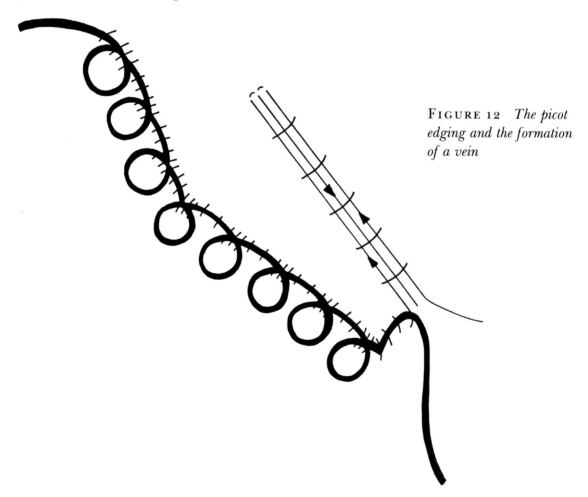

FIGURE 12 *The picot edging and the formation of a vein*

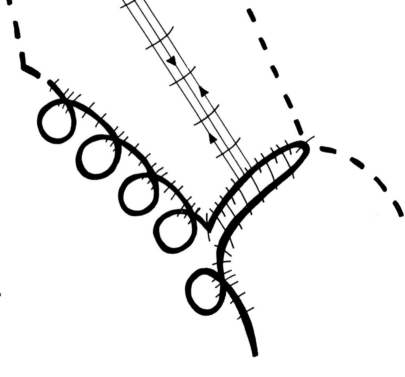

FIGURE 13 *After the completion of the vein, work on the coarse thread outline is resumed*

FIGURE 14 *Securing the coarse threads when two lie side by side*

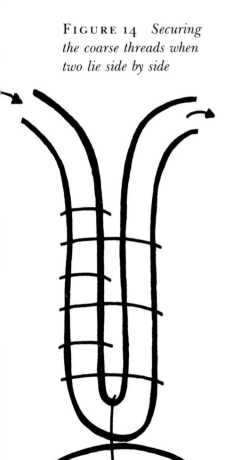

11 and 12 When the line dividing the top left and bottom left petals is reached, work the two coarse threads side by side, stitching over both coarse threads (FIGURE 14). Complete the top left petal.

13 and 14 Work the top right petal and part of the lower right petal, following the arrows.

15 Complete the inner edge of the right-hand leaf.

16 From the leaf point work along the short outer edges to B and then along the outer edge to C.

Step 6

(A) The ball of coarse thread should still be attached to the lace, it having been used to work all but the outer edge of the design. Prepare to make the picots, which are the decorative circles or loops of coarse thread which form the traditional Carrickmacross Lace edging. Picots are not worked on the edge which is sewn to the handkerchief.

(B) With the fine thread, work two or three oversewing stitches to anchor the coarse thread before making the first picot.

(C) To make a picot, curve the coarse thread clockwise, and where the thread overlaps at the base of the picot make one stitch with the fine thread to hold the loop in place.

(D) Pull up the coarse thread forming the picot so that a tiny circle is created. A knitting needle or cocktail stick is useful in gauging these circles. A NO 13 (2.5 mm) knitting needle was used for this corner.

(E) Make two extra stitches by the side of the one already made, within the circle of the picot (FIGURE 15).

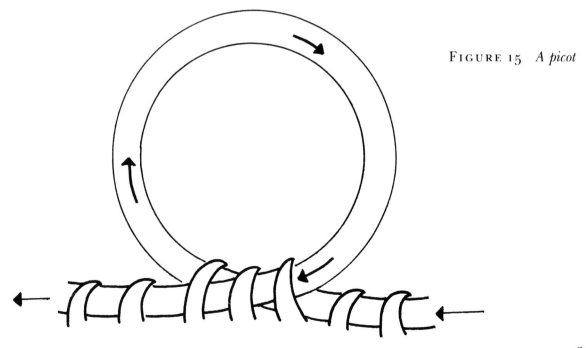

FIGURE 15 *A picot*

(F) Continue oversewing approximately two stitches between each carefully formed picot. Ensure that all picots are uniform in size and shape.

In this sample the picots and the lower outer edges are worked simultaneously. Sometimes in a large piece of lace the outer edge is first outlined with coarse thread and the picots are added afterwards, giving the lace a double edge and greater strength.

Step 7

(A) When the picots are finished, before working the last two or three oversewing stitches, cut the coarse thread, leaving approximately 8 cm (3 in). This end should then be pulled through all the layers to the back of the work.

(B) Secure the ends of the coarse thread with three tightly pulled stitches. Make the joins as unobtrusive as possible.

(C) For a neat finish, leave the end of the coarse thread hanging at the back of the work. Cut off the coarse thread when all work and fillings have been completed.

Step 8

(A) With the point of a needle, lift a small part of the organdie, separating it from the net beneath.

(B) Snip a hole large enough to insert the rounded blade of the scissors.

(C) Cut away the organdie, close to the coarse thread at the edge of the design. Great care must be taken not to cut either the stitching or the net.

(D) The net that is revealed may be decorated with net embroidery stitches known as 'fillings'. Instructions for working seven different fillings are given in the next chapter.

(E) The 'pops' are worked in buttonhole stitch as described on page 47.

Step 9

Once the pops and fillings have been completed remove the tacking threads; the lace is then ready to be mounted on to a handkerchief square.

(A)   Cut round the outer edges of the lace, trimming away the surplus net and organdie but leaving 3 mm (⅛ in) along the top scalloped edge. This is the edge that will be attached to the handkerchief, and leaving this tiny border will prevent the net and organdie from pulling away from the oversewn coarse thread when (plain) buttonhole-stitching.

(B)   Place the completed lace across one corner of the handkerchief square. Put the wrong side of the Carrickmacross against the right side of the handkerchief.

(C)   Tack into place. Tack across the top of the leaves and beneath the scallops.

(D)   With the right side facing, work (plain) buttonhole stitch along the outer edge of the broad top band, stitching through organdie, net and handkerchief *over* and *round* the coarse thread. Small, closely spaced stitches will result in a neat and secure join.

(E)   Oversew or (plain) buttonhole stitch the inner line of the top band. Stitch through all layers as before (FIGURE 16).

FIGURE 16
Completing the handkerchief corner: mounting the lace

(F)   Turn the work so that the wrong side is facing. Cut the handkerchief corner from the square, cutting as close to the lace as possible.

—4—

FILLINGS

he fillings, or net embroidery stitches, must complement the designs; when selecting and devising the seven fillings described in this section we were very conscious of that fact. A simple filling is often an effective filling and, for that reason, relatively uncomplicated net embroidery stitches have been included.

Some lacemakers state that fillings should be worked after the lace has been removed from the pattern. Caution must be exercised here because, if that instruction is followed, it is much more difficult to complete the filling successfully, as the lace then lacks the support provided by the tracing paper pattern. It is therefore suggested that all fillings are worked before the Carrickmacross is taken off the tracing paper.

It is often useful to practise the stitches by attaching a piece of net to a dark-coloured paper. It is then easy to see where to push in the needle and how the stitches look. It helps to use the eye of the needle, or a ballpoint needle, when working the fillings, buttonhole bars, thorns and pops.

There are numerous net fillings which are suitable for Carrickmacross Lace and any reliable needlework book will give instructions as to how to do them. Some are extremely complex but well worth trying. Several of the fillings explained here are standard net fillings while others are adaptations devised specially. None of them is too difficult for anyone who takes care to follow the diagrams. The lacemaker may even wish to vary the fillings by including, for example, additional rows of running or darning stitches and alternating them with the more elaborate lines of filling stitches. With a little ingenuity every filling can be made to look different and distinctive. It is exciting to experiment.

N.B. The dotted line indicates the needle travelling behind the work.

Filling 1

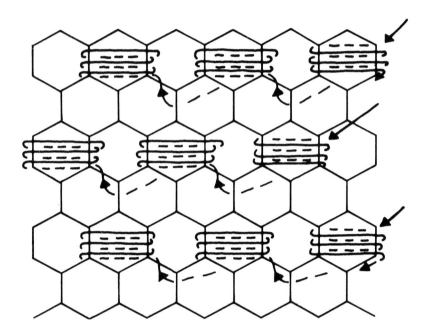

FIGURE 17 *Filling 1:*
method of work

This was the filling used in the lace handkerchief described in the previous chapter (FIGURE 3).

FIRST ROW
Start on the right of the section to be filled.

Work three stitches *under* and *over* one space of net. (Two bars of net equal one space.)

When the last of the three stitches has been worked take the needle down the back of the work *under* one vertical bar and *over* one diagonal bar (FIGURE 18). The thread is then correctly positioned to start the next block of three stitches. (This method hides the thread when travelling from one group of stitches to another.)

SECOND ROW

Leave one row of net unworked.

Work blocks of three *under* and *over* stitches in the spaces between the blocks of stitches in the first row.

Continue to stitch, alternating rows, until the space available has been completely decorated.

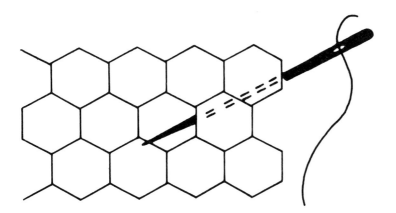

FIGURE 18 *Filling 1: positioning the needle*

Filling 2

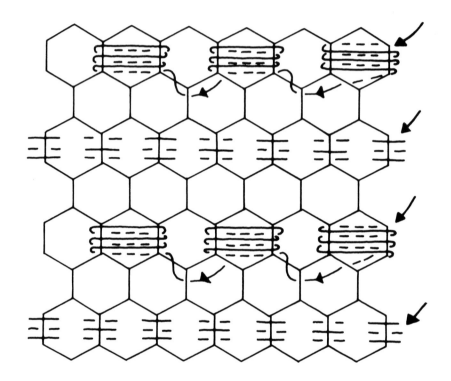

FIGURE 19   *Filling 2:*
method of work

FIRST ROW

Beginning on the right, work a block of three *under* and *over* stitches, as for Filling 1.

SECOND ROW

Leave one row of net unworked.

Work three rows of darning stitches *under* and *over* one bar of net.

Repeat first and second rows as required.

FIGURE 20 *Pattern for the second handkerchief corner*

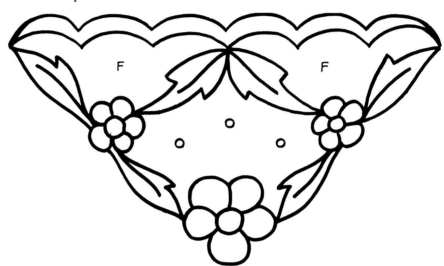

FIGURE 21 *The second pattern completed, using filling 2*

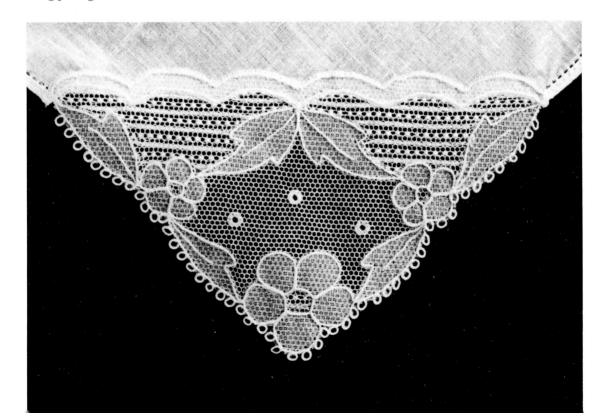

Filling 3

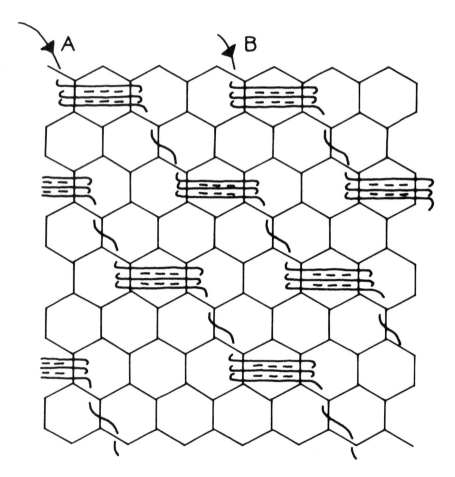

FIGURE 22 *Filling 3:*
method of work

FIRST ROW
Start at A on the left of the work. These stitches are worked diagonally across the net.

Work *over* and *under* one space of net, three times.

Carry the thread *under*, *over* and *under* the bars, in a diagonal direction to the right, ready to start the second block of stitches. Continue each block in the same diagonal direction.

FIGURE 23 *Pattern for the third handkerchief corner*

SECOND ROW

Start at B, leaving one bar of net between each block of three stitches. Work diagonally as in the first row.

Continue.

FIGURE 24 *The third pattern completed, using filling 3*

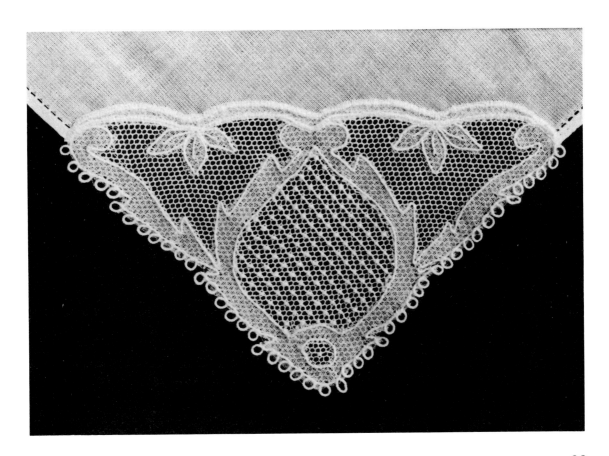

Filling 4

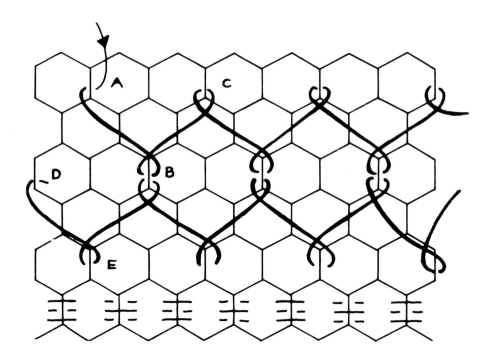

FIGURE 25 *Filling 4:*
method of work

FIRST ROW

Start on the left at A.

Pass the needle *under* one bar of net from right to left.

Miss one row of net and work diagonally down to B.

Pass the needle from right to left *under* one bar of net.

Work diagonally up to C.

Pass the needle from right to left *under* one bar of net, as before, forming elongated figures-of-eight.

Continue across the row.

SECOND ROW

When commencing the second row begin at the point marked D.

Following the procedures already described, work diagonally to E, and continue.

THIRD ROW

Work three rows of darning stitches *over* and *under* bars of
net across the row.

Repeat all three rows.

FIGURE 26 *Pattern*
for the fourth
handkerchief corner

FIGURE 27 *The fourth*
pattern completed, using
filling 4

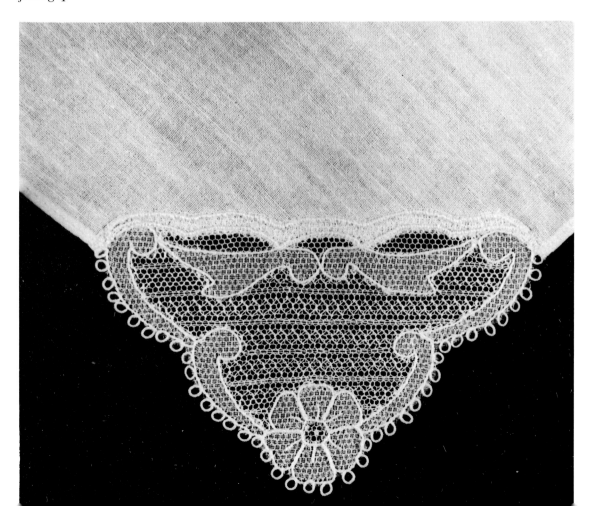

Filling 5

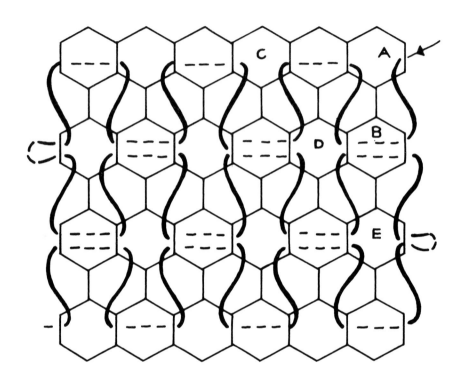

FIGURE 28 *Filling 5:*
method of work

FIRST ROW

Start on the right by passing a needle and thread *under* one bar of net into the space marked A.

Take the needle and thread down to the right of space B, missing one row.

Pass the needle *under* two bars, from right to left, into the space D, and then up to space A.

Work from right to left *under* two bars to space C, and down again to space D.

Continue.

FIGURE 29 *Pattern for the fifth handkerchief corner*

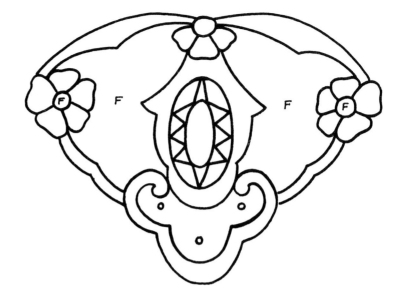

FIGURE 30 *The fifth pattern completed, using filling 5*

Filling 6

FIGURE 31   *Filling 6:*
method of work

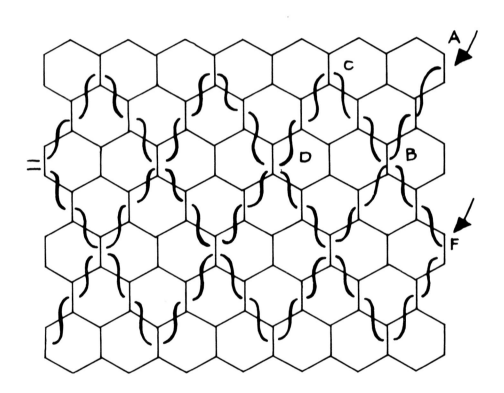

FIRST ROW
Start on the right at A.

Work *under, over, under, over* four single diagonal bars to the space B.

From B take the needle and thread *under, over, under, over* diagonally to C.

Work to D, repeating the first step.

Continue.

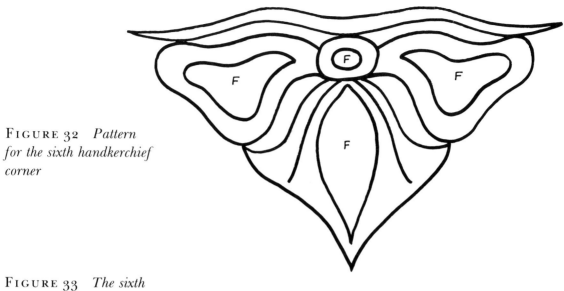

FIGURE 32 *Pattern for the sixth handkerchief corner*

FIGURE 33 *The sixth pattern completed, using filling 6*

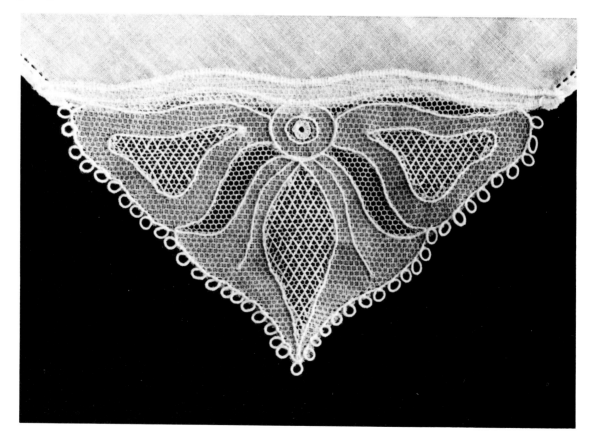

Filling 7

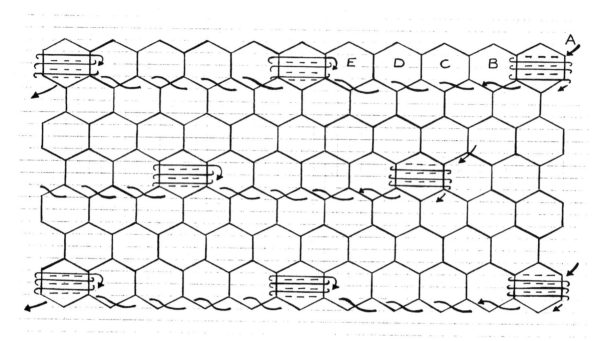

FIGURE 34 *Filling 7:*
method of work

FIRST ROW

Start on the right at the point marked A.

Make a block of three *under* and *over* stitches *over* two bars.

Take the needle down the back of the work and weave the thread over the base bars of spaces B, C, D and E, ready to start the next block of stitches. (This method is used to conceal the threads as already described in Filling 1.)

SECOND ROW

After leaving two rows of net unworked commence the second row.

Position the blocks of stitches to form the pattern, as in the diagram. (This filling is ideal for large spaces and examples of it can be seen in designs such as the 'Lily' [FIGURE 61] and 'Mary' [FIGURE 93].)

Pops *(Figures 35 AND 36)*

Pops are small circles of buttonhole stitches. Two of them are worked in the centre of the first handkerchief corner design (FIGURE 3).

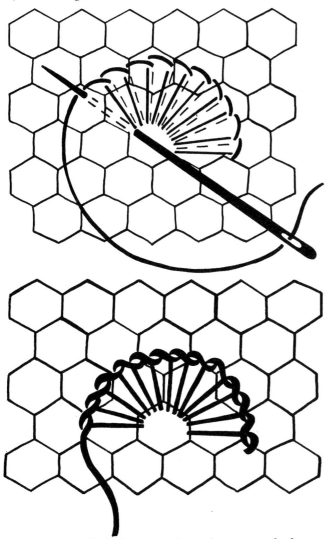

FIGURE 35 *A pop: work in progress*

FIGURE 36 *A partially completed pop*

The needle is inserted into the centre hole, passing under two bars of net (observe the dotted line indicated on the diagram labelled 'Work in progress') and back over two bars of net (the solid or unbroken line indicates this part of the process).

Continue buttonholing until a neatly formed pop has been made.

Bars and Thorns

The handkerchief corner described in the step-by-step instructions is an example of Carrickmacross 'appliqué work'. In 'guipure' Carrickmacross both the net *and* the organdie are cut away. The spaces left are filled with buttonhole bars and thorns.

Bars are worked across a space in the design from which the net and the organdie are later cut out. The cutting out must be done *after* the buttonhole bars have been completed. Fine thread is used to work the bars. One strand is taken three times across the space. The threads must lie closely side by side. Buttonhole stitches are then worked over the three threads.

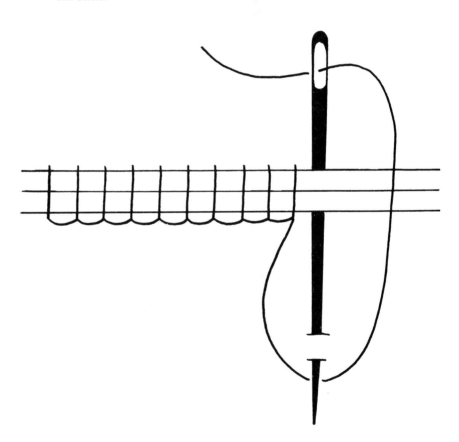

FIGURE 37
Forming a thorn

FIGURE 38 *A partially worked bar and thorn*

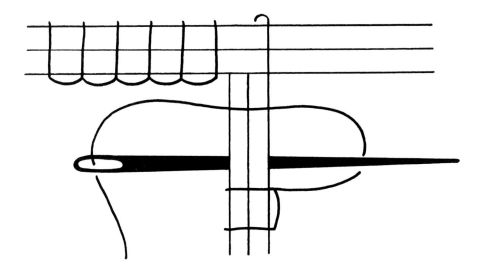

Thorns take their name from thorns in nature which protrude from the stem. In Carrickmacross they are added part way along a bar. Push the needle under a bar as when forming buttonhole stitch. Pick up two threads of organdie 3 mm (⅛ in) away from the bar (FIGURE 37). Pull out the needle to form a long three-thread buttonhole stitch. Work approximately three buttonhole stitches over these threads (FIGURE 38) to produce a thorn. Continue buttonholing over the rest of the bar.

The Designs

ood design is a harmonious blend of the practical and the aesthetic. That statement is also applicable to Carrickmacross. The lace design must be workable, fit for its intended purpose and pleasing to the eye.

There are few rules when designing for Carrickmacross, but it is useful to observe certain guidelines. When adapting patterns or, when frustration caused by the difficulty of finding a suitable design forces the lacemaker to pick up his or her own pen, these hints may help:

1 Too many holes (guipure work) produce not only a fragile design but a fragile piece of lace. The function the lace will serve must be considered carefully. It is no use, for instance, spending hours making a collar so delicate that it cannot be worn or washed.

2 A border round the edge of the lace adds both strength and definition. In lace intended as a picture a border is unnecessary, as the frame provides the definition and the backing board the strength.

3 Attention can be drawn to a focal point of the lace by creating areas for fillings, for example in the points of a collar or in the central motif of a mat.

4 Too many fillings often result in a richly ornamented but cluttered appearance. Again, careful consideration should be given to the use of the finished lace.

5 Simple, bold lines of design often work best, certainly when one is experimenting.

Almost any theme can be used as a basis for Carrickmacross design. Smooth, flowing lines are advocated, first because they are aesthetically pleasing and, next, because they are easy to work. Sharp angles create problems when securing the thread, when endeavouring to maintain a neat point and when cutting out.

Traditional Carrickmacross is full of swirls and curves, the source of inspiration often being nature. In contrast, poor design is wooden, with a minimum of movement, and for that reason straight, hard lines do not seem compatible with this type of lace.

The designs in this book cover a wide and diverse range with, hopefully, something to please all tastes. The creative lacemaker may see potential in a mat which could become a framed picture or part of a wall hanging. A nursery picture such as 'Sleeping Beauty' (FIGURE 68) could be stitched to a nightdress case. 'Little Red Riding Hood' (FIGURE 65) could easily become part of a frieze, either behind glass or mounted on unframed fabric. 'The Magi Lantern' (FIGURE 102) would make an equally attractive scene if used flat. Even the motifs used as page decorations could be adapted to make interesting pieces of lace.

To enable these page decorations to be correctly termed 'Carrickmacross', spaces need to be created from which the organdie can be cut away so that the net underneath can be filled with net embroidery stitches.

Other changes could be made when adapting these motifs; for example, another line drawn round a bud, a petal or a leaf will make it possible to cut away the centre entirely, creating a guipure to be filled with buttonhole bars. Alternatively, the organdie alone could be removed and the net filled in the traditional way. Treated in these ways the motifs can be used for greeting cards, as pictures or under paperweights. They can also be added to an item of clothing.

If a design is to be oversewn to a garment, picots should not, of course, be used. Picots can be worked if the lace is a temporary ornamentation when no oversewing is necessary. The lace can be attached with a few securing stitches to, perhaps, the lapel of a velvet or brocade jacket. It can then be removed without damaging either lace or garment.

The designs can be as versatile as the lacemaker who uses them.

Handkerchief Corners

Seven handkerchief corner designs have been included. Correctly mounted they make very acceptable gifts and, being small, they are an ideal way of learning the craft.

The letter 'F' in six of the corner designs marks a suitable space for a filling, as illustrated in FIGURES 2, 20, 23, 26, 29, 32 and in the accompanying photographs (FIGURES 3, 21, 24, 27, 30, 33).

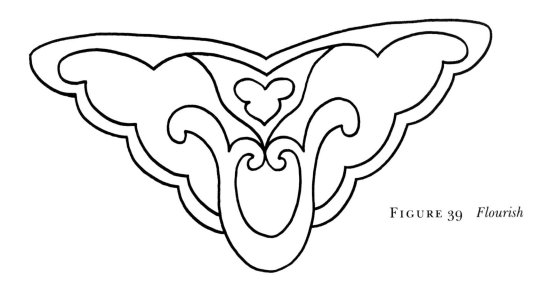

FIGURE 39 *Flourish*

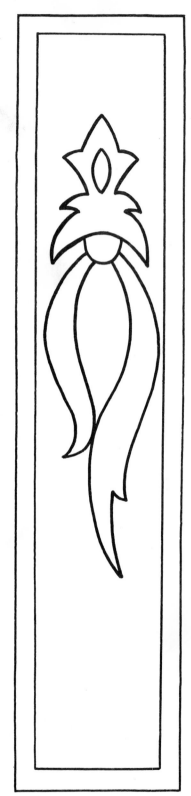

FIGURE 40 *Valour*

Bookmarks

Like the handkerchief corners, bookmarks such as 'Valour' (FIGURE 40) and 'Oak' (FIGURES 41 and 42) are relatively easy to make and provide the novice with an interesting project during which the basic skills can be practised.

The Staffordshire or Stafford Knot and the oak leaves in 'Oak' are emblems much seen on objects originating in that county. The oak leaves commemorate the escape of King Charles II after the Battle of Worcester in 1650. The story of how he was concealed in a massive oak tree is well-known in Staffordshire.

FIGURE 41   *Oak*

FIGURE 42   *Oak*

Mats

These are always popular with crafts men and women, probably because they can be used in so many different ways and usually need neither fabric nor frame, nor any sort of mount, to make them complete.

The designs range from the more simple ('Friendship' [FIGURE 43], 'Charm' [FIGURES 44 and 45], 'Garland' [FIGURE 46]) with few fillings and pops, to the more complex ('Acorn' [FIGURE 47], 'Acanthus' [FIGURES 48 and 49], 'Corinth' [FIGURE 50], 'Festoon' [FIGURES 51 and 52], 'Carnation', [FIGURE 53], 'Convolvulus' [FIGURES 56 and 57]).

'Charm' was specially designed for beginners because it is possible to complete the inner and outer edges with only two lengths of coarse thread, thus reducing the number of joins.

The large space in the centre of 'Acorn' is suitable for filling No. 7 (page 46).

FIGURE 43   *Friendship*

FIGURE 44   *Charm*

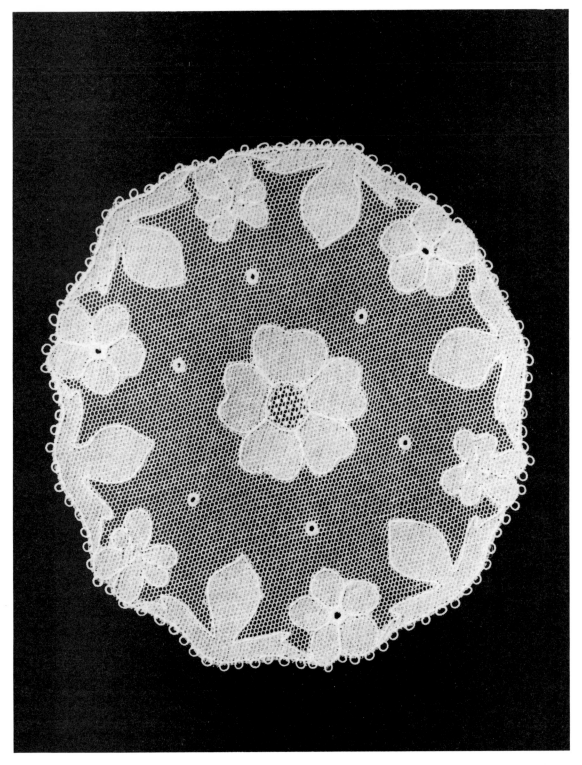

FIGURE 45 *Charm*

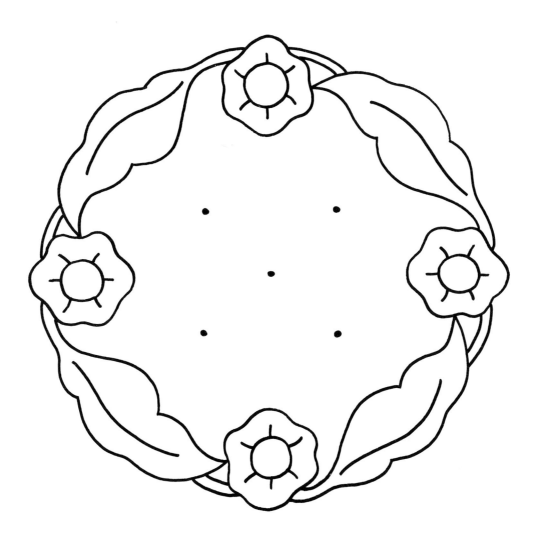

FIGURE 46　*Garland*

FIGURE 47   *Acorn*

FIGURE 48 *Acanthus:
a pleasing blend of the
asymmetrical and the
symmetrical, designed to
allow the lacemaker to
experiment with a variety
of fillings*

61

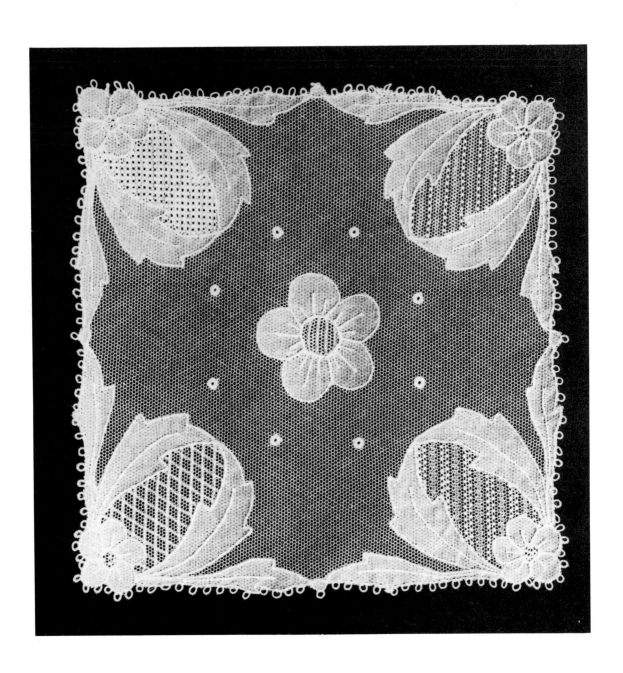

FIGURE 49   *Acanthus*

F I G U R E 50 *Corinth*

FIGURE 51 *Festoon*

FIGURE 52   *Festoon*

FIGURE 53 *Carnation*

FIGURE 54 *Loyal*

FIGURE 55 *Loyal*

FIGURE 56
Convolvulus

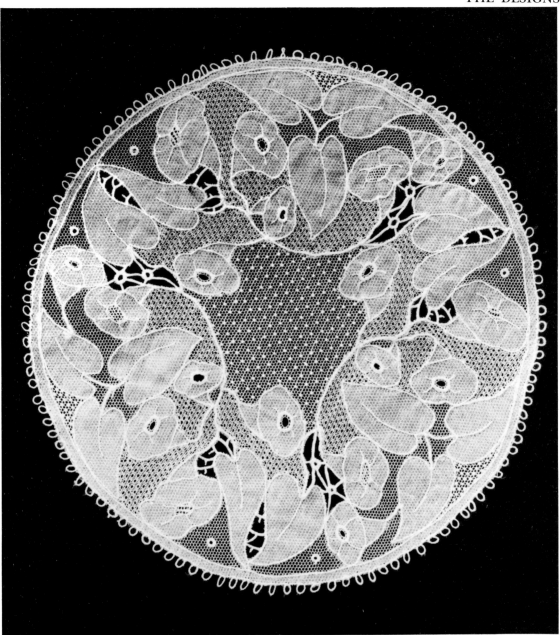

FIGURE 57
Convolvulus. Here can be
seen an example of both
'appliqué' and 'guipure'
lace, showing the
traditional bars and
thorns which are much
used in 'guipure'

69

FIGURE 58 *Idyll*
(increase by 5%)

'Idyll' [F I G U R E 58] is an asymmetrical design which, if not used as a mat, could be suspended from the pointed corner and hung in a window, or in a well-illuminated part of a room.

The veins down every petal in 'Idyll' are functional because they hold down the organdie which sometimes wrinkles over large spaces if not anchored securely. It should be noted that similar design lines which represent not only veins but such things as folds, crease marks, strands of hair, bark on trees and even flying birds, all serve the same purpose. It is therefore important to include them. Discretion, however, should be used as to whether these 'veins' should be worked as traditional veins following the instructions given in the step-by-step guidelines (page 27) or merely treated as an extension of the coarse thread outline.

Pictures

Some designs, such as 'Pansy' (FIGURE 59) and 'Lily' (FIGURES 60 and 61), could be used for either mats or pictures, though both 'Ascent' (FIGURE 62) and 'Fuchsia' (FIGURE 63) are intended to be framed.

An extra border line, parallel to that already drawn round 'Fuchsia', will create a solid edging of net and organdie if that is required and picots are desired. If framed, such a border is, of course, not essential.

The eye of the mouse in 'Ascent' is a pop. The whiskers are worked as veins.

FIGURE 59 *Pansy*

FIGURE 60   *Lily*

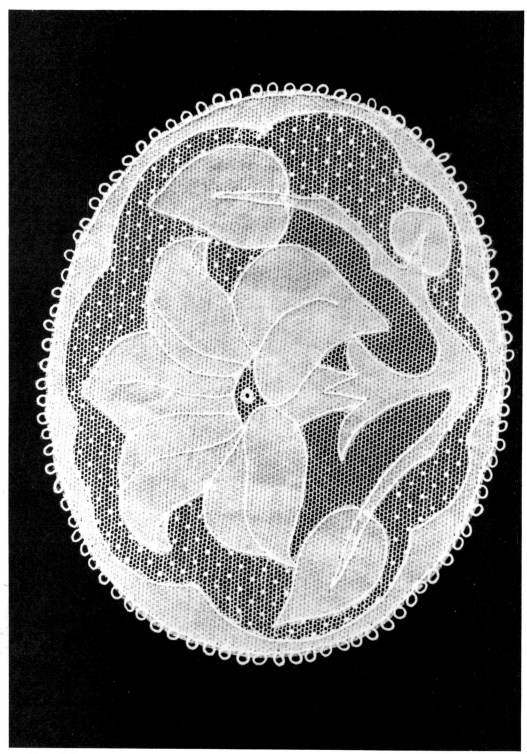

FIGURE 61   *Lily*

FIGURE 62   *Ascent*

FIGURE 63 *Fuchsia*

76

FIGURE 64 *Sunrise*

Nursery or Story-Book Pictures

These should delight any child and are great fun to work. As already explained in Chapter 5, they can be treated in a variety of ways.

An alternative design for the geese in 'Goose Girl' has been included. (FIGURE 70). The additional pair could be used instead of, or as well as, the originals and provides spaces for fillings in the wings.

FIGURE 65
Little Red Riding Hood

FIGURE 66
Little Red Riding Hood

FIGURE 67
Enchanted Castle

FIGURE 68
Sleeping Beauty

FIGURE 69　*Goose Girl*

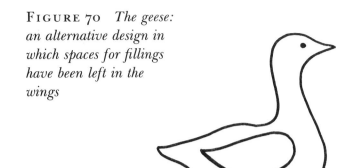

FIGURE 70 *The geese:
an alternative design in
which spaces for fillings
have been left in the
wings*

FIGURE 71
Goose Girl

FIGURE 72 *Genie*

FIGURE 73 *Mermaid*

FIGURE 74 *Boot House*

FIGURE 75 *Fairytale Betrothal*

Edgings, Ornamentation and Insertions

'Flamboyant' (FIGURE 77) is an edging for a circular mat which could have a plain linen centre.

Both 'Harebell' (FIGURE 76) and 'Forget-Me-Not' (FIGURE 78) could be used as edgings for wedding veils, or as trimmings for baby or ceremonial gowns. 'Forget-Me-Not' can be seen on the cushion in FIGURE 79.

The flowers in 'Harebell' are worked with one row of coarse thread in a continuous line from the base of the stem, which emerges from the leaf, to the petal tip, and from the petal tip back to the base of the stem. This produces a double stem which adds strength when cutting out.

The bells and bow from the 'Fairytale Betrothal' (FIGURE 75) could also be used to decorate an appropriate veil or dress.

Close inspection of motifs used as page decorations in this book will reveal that these, too, could be employed very effectively. Suggestions as to how this can be done have been given in Chapter 5.

'Dog Rose' (FIGURE 80) and 'Legend' (FIGURE 81) are both insertions (a border or band of lace let into fabric) and like the edgings can be extended by repeating the pattern until the desired length is reached, as indicated by the dotted lines.

FIGURE 76   *Harebell*

FIGURE 77
*Flamboyant: to complete
the circle, trace twice,
reverse one tracing and
align the halves*

FIGURE 78
Forget-me-not

FIGURE 79 *The*
Forget-me-not cushion

FIGURE 80 *Dog Rose*

FIGURE 81 *Legend*

FIGURE 83   *Dewdrop*

Collars

Lace collars have been an important fashion accessory for centuries, although their popularity fluctuates and styles vary. Different types of neckline were considered when designing the ones in this book.

'Dewdrop' (FIGURES 82 and 83), the points of which should not meet, is suitable for a lower neckline. The two tear shapes mid-way along the collar could be cut out completely after working the bars.

FIGURE 82   *Dewdrop*

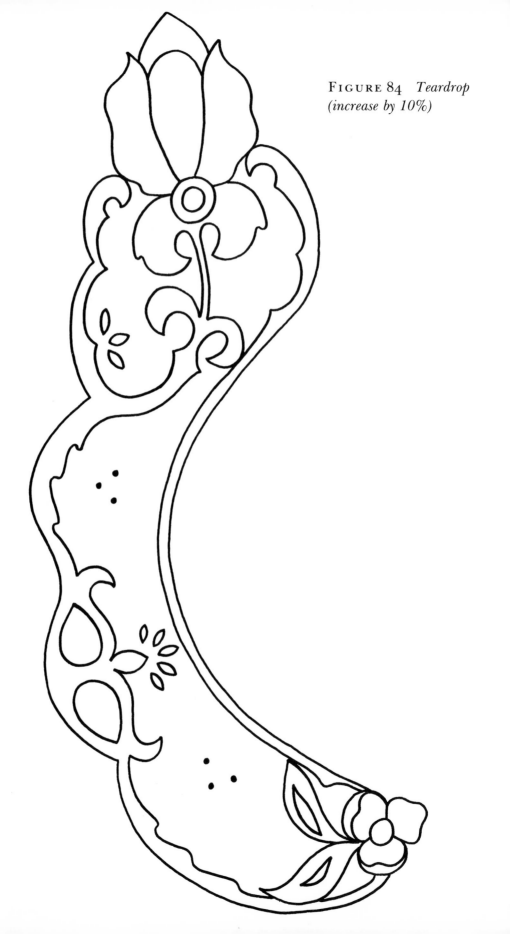

FIGURE 84 *Teardrop*
(increase by 10%)

In 'Teardrop' (FIGURE 84), an adaptation of 'Dewdrop', the points of the collar curve out and down, in the usual way, to allow the points to meet.

'Daisy' (FIGURES 85 and 86) is an example of traditional Carrickmacross Lace, with scrolls and daisies forming a 'Peter Pan' collar. There are spaces for fillings inside the scrolls. The stems are worked with two rows of coarse thread.

FIGURE 85 *Daisy*

FIGURE 86 *Daisy: the extra daisy at the back allows the collar to overlap for a neat fit*

'Bud' (FIGURE 87) is designed for a small amount of work. There are spaces for fillings on either side of the central leaf spray. A place for zig-zag bars has been marked, and for pops, too.

FIGURE 87 *Bud*

FIGURE 88 *Cuckoo Pint fan (reduced in size to show the whole design)*

Fans

Often collected, and much admired, fans are a challenge to make and mount, but very much worth the effort. Care must be taken to leave sufficient fabric to enable the completed fan to be attached to its supporting framework. Picots should only be worked along the top edge.

FIGURE 89 *Cuckoo Pint: a little more than half the design for the fan is shown here. (The vertical, symmetrical flower is in the centre.) Trace and align the halves. (Increase by 10%)*

FIGURE 90   *Butterfly*
fan: trace and align the
halves. The bottom
butterfly marks the centre
point. (Increase by 10%)

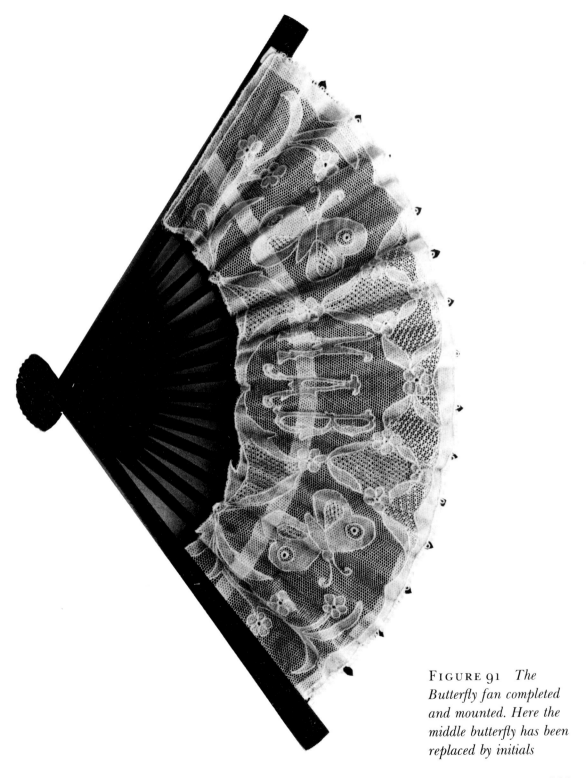

FIGURE 91 *The Butterfly fan completed and mounted. Here the middle butterfly has been replaced by initials*

Cards

'Mary' (FIGURES 92 and 93), 'Snow-biz-man' (FIGURE 94) and 'Candle' (FIGURE 95) all represent seasonal themes, while 'Vase' (FIGURE 96) and 'Celebration' (FIGURE 97) would create a greeting card suitable for several occasions. The decorative page motifs, or parts of them, could also be used in this way, as could the designs for 'The Magi Lantern' (FIGURES 98–101).

It is hoped that Mrs Grey Porter would have approved.

FIGURE 92 *Mary*

FIGURE 93   *Mary*

FIGURE 94
Snow-biz-man

FIGURE 95   *Candle*

FIGURE 96   *Vase*

FIGURE 97
Celebration

FIGURE 98
The Magi (1)

FIGURE 99
The Magi (2)

FIGURE 101
The Star (4)

FIGURE 100
The Magi (3)

FIGURE 102   *The Magi lantern*

SUPPLIERS AND SOURCES OF INFORMATION

GENERAL SUPPLIERS:

United Kingdom

Alby Lace Museum
Cromer Road
Alby
Norfolk NR11 7QE

Busy Bobbins
Unit 7
Scarrots Lane
Newport
IOW PO30 1JD

Chosen Crafts Centre
46 Winchcombe Street
Cheltenham
Glos GL52 2ND

Jo Firth
Lace Marketing & Needlecraft
  Supplies
58 Kent Crescent
Lowtown
Pudsey
W Yorks LS28 9EB

J. & J. Ford
October Hill
Upper Way
Upper Longdon
Rugeley
Staffs WS15 1QB

Framecraft
83 Hampstead Road
Handsworth Wood
Birmingham B2 1JA

Doreen Gill
14 Barnfield Road
Petersfield
Hants GU31 4DQ

R. Gravestock
Highwood
Crews Hill
Alfrick
Worcs WR6 5HF

The Handicraft Shop
47 Northgate
Canterbury
Kent CT1 1BE

Frank Herring & Sons
27 High West Street
Dorchester
Dorset DT1 1UP

Honiton Lace Shop
44 High Street
Honiton
Devon

D. J. Hornsby
149 High Street
Burton Latimer
Kettering
Northants NN15 5RL
also at:
25 Manwood Avenue
Canterbury
Kent CT2 7AH

Frances Iles
73 High Street
Rochester
Kent ME1 1LX

Jane's Pincushions
Unit 4
Taverham Crafts
Taverham Nursery Centre
Fir Covert Road
Taverham
Norwich NR8 6HT

Loricraft
19 Peregrine Way
Grove
Wantage
Oxon

Needlestyle
5 The Woolmead
Farnham
Surrey GU9 7TX

Needlestyle
24–26 West Street
Alresford
Hants

Needlework
Ann Bartlee
Bucklers Farm
Coggeshall
Essex CO6 1SB

Needle and Thread
80 High Street
Horsell
Woking
Surrey GU21 4SZ

The Needlewoman
21 Needless Alley
off New Street
Birmingham B2 5AE

T. Parker (mail order)
124 Corhampton Road
Boscombe East
Bournemouth
Dorset BH6 5NZ

Jane Playford
North Lodge
Church Close
West Runton
Norfolk NR27 9QY

Redburn Crafts
Squires Garden Centre
Halliford Road
Upper Halliford
Shepperton
Middx TW17 8RU

Christine Riley
53 Barclay Street
Stonehaven
Kincardineshire
Scotland

Peter & Beverley Scarlett
Strupak, Hill Head
Cold Wells, Ellon
Grampian, Scotland

Ken & Pat Schultz
134 Wisbech Road
Thornley
Peterborough

J. S. Sear
Lacecraft Supplies
8 Hill View
Sherrington
Bucks MK16 9NY

Sebalace
Waterloo Mills
Howden Road
Silsden
W Yorks BD2 0NA

A. Sells
49 Pedley Lane
Clifton
Shefford
Beds

Shireburn Lace
Finkle Court
Finkle Hill
Sherburn in Elmet
N Yorks LS25 6EB

SMP
4 Garners Close
Chalfont St Peter
Bucks SL9 0HB

Southern Handicrafts
20 Kensington Gardens
Brighton
Sussex BN1 4AC

Spangles
Carole Morris
Burwell
Cambs CB5 0ED

Stitches
Dovehouse Shopping Parade
Warwick Road
Olton
Solihull
W Midlands

Teazle Embroideries
35 Boothferry Road
Hull
N Humberside

Lynn Turner
Church Meadow Crafts
15 Carisbrooke Drive
Winsford
Cheshire CW7 1LN

Valley House Craft Studios
Ruston
Scarborough
N Yorks

George Walker
The Corner Shop
Rickinghall
Diss
Norfolk

West End Lace Supplies
Ravensworth Court Road
Mortimer West End
Reading
Berks RG7 3UD

George White Lacemakers' Supplies
40 Heath Drive
Boston Spa
W Yorks L23 6PB

BOBBINS

A. R. Arches
The Poplars
Shetland
near Stowmarket
Suffolk IP14 3DE

T. Brown
Temple Lane Cottage
Littledean
Cinderford
Glos

Chrisken Bobbins
26 Cedar Drive
Kingsclere
Bucks RG15 8TD

Malcolm J. Fielding
2 Northern Terrace
Moss Lane
Silverdale
Lancs LA5 0ST

Richard Gravestock
Highwood
Crews Hill
Alfrick
Worcs WR6 5HF

Larkfield Crafts
Hilary Rickitts
4 Island Cottages
Mapledurwell
Basingstoke
Hants RG25 2LU

Loricraft
19 Peregrine Way
Grove
Wantage
Oxon

T. Parker
124 Corhampton Road
Boscombe East
Bournemouth
Dorset BH6 5NZ

Bryan Phillips
Pantglas
Cellan
Lampeter
Dyfed SA48 8JD

D. H. Shaw
47 Lamor Crescent
Thrushcroft
S Yorks S66 9QD

Sizelands
1 Highfield Road
Winslow
Bucks MK10 3QU

Christine & David Springett
21 Hillmorton Road
Rugby
War CV22 5DF

Richard Viney
Unit 7
Port Royal Street
Southsea
Hants PO5 3UD

West End Lace Suppliers
Ravensworth Court Road
Mortimer West End
Reading
Berks RG7 3UD

LACE PILLOWS

Newnham Lace Equipment
15 Marlowe Close
Basingstoke
Hants RG24 9DD

BOOKS

Christopher Williams
19 Morrison Avenue
Parkstone
Poole
Dorset BH17 4AD

SILK EMBROIDERY AND LACE THREAD

E. & J. Piper
Silverlea
Flax Lane
Glemsford
Suffolk CO10 7RS

SILK WEAVING YARN

Hilary Chetwynd
Kipping Cottage
Cheriton
Alresford
Hants SO24 0PW

FRAMES AND MOUNTS

Doreen Campbell
Highcliff
Brenisham Road
Malmesbury
Wilts

MATT COLOURED TRANSPARENT ADHESIVE FILM

Heffers Graphic Shop
26 King Street
Cambridge CB1 1LN

LINEN
by the metre (yard)
and made up articles
of church linen

Mary Collins
Church Furnishings
St Andrews Hall
Humber Doucy Lane
Ipswich
Suffolk IP4 3BP

Hayes and Finch
Head Office & Factory
Hanson Road
Aintree
Liverpool L9 9BP

CARRICKMACROSS

Joan Kelly
39 Copeland Avenue
Tittensor
Stoke-on-Trent
Staffs ST12 9JA

Lichfield Needlework Centre
5 St John Street
Lichfield
Staffs WS13 6NU

Mace & Nairn
89 Crane Street
Salisbury
Wilts SP1 2PY

Dorothy Pearce
5 Fulshaw Avenue
Wimslow
Cheshire SK9 5JA

Janet Smith
77 Falmouth Avenue
Weeping Cross
Stafford
ST17 0JG

United States of America

Arbor House
22 Arbor Lane
Roslyn Hights
NY 11577

Baltazor Inc.
3262 Severn Avenue
Metairie
LA 7002

Beggars' Lace
P.O. Box 17263
Denver
Colo 80217

Berga Ullman Inc.
P.O. Box 918
North Adams
MA 01247

Frederick J. Fawcett
129 South Street
Boston
MA 02130

Frivolité
15526 Densmore N.
Seattle
WA 98113

Happy Hands
3007 S. W. Marshall
Pendleton
Oreg 97180

International Old Lacers
P.O. Box 1029
Westminster
Colo 80030

Lace Place de Belgique
800 S. W. 17th Street
Boca Raton
FL 33432

Lacis
2150 Stuart Street
Berkeley
CA 9470

Robin's Bobbins
RTL Box 1736
Mineral Bluff
GA 30559

Robin and Russ
Handweavers
533 North Adams Street
McMinnvills
Oreg 97128

Some Place
2990 Adline Street
Berkeley
CA 94703

Osma G. Todd Studio
319 Mendoza Avenue
Coral Gables
FL 33134

The Unique And Art Lace Cleaners
5926 Delman Boulevard
St Louis
MO 63112

Van Scriver Bobbin Lace
130 Cascadilla Park
Ithaca
NY 14850

The World in Stitches
82 South Street
Milford
N.H. 03055

Australia

Dentelles Lace Supplies
3 Narrak Close
Jindalee
Queensland 4074

The Lacemaker
94 Fordham Avenue
Hartwell
Victoria 3124

Spindle and Loom
Arcade 83
Longueville Road
Lane Cove
NSW 2066

Tulis Crafts
201 Avoca Street
Randwick
NSW 2031

Belgium

't Handwekhuisje
Katelijnestraat 23
8000 Bruges

Kantcentrum
Balstraat 14
8000 Bruges

Manufacture Belge de Dentelle
6 Galerie de la Reine
Galeries Royales St Hubert
1000 Bruxelles

Orchidée
Mariastraat 18
8000 Bruges

Ann Thys
't Apostelientje
Balstraat 11
8000 Bruges

France

Centre d'Initiations à la Dentelle du
  Puy
2 Rue Duguesclin
43000 Le Puy en Velay

A L'Econome
Anne-Marie Deydier
Ecole de Dentelle aux Fuseaux
10 rue Paul Chenavard
6901 Lyon

Rougier and Plé
13–15 bd des Filles de Calvaire
75003 Paris

West Germany

Der Fenster Laden
Berliner Str. 8
D 6483 Bad Soden
Salmünster

P.P. Hempel
Ortolanweg 34
1000 Berlin 47

Heikona De Ruijter
Kleoppelgrosshandel
Langer Steinweg 38
D4933 Blomberg

Holland

Blokker's Boektiek
Bronsteeweg 4/4a
2101 AC Heemstede

Theo Brejaat
Postbus 5199
3008 AD Rotterdam

Magazijn *De Vlijt*
Lijnmarkt 48
Utrecht

Switzerland

Fadehax
Inh. Irene Solca
4105 Biel-Benken
Basel

New Zealand

Peter McLeavey
P.O. Box 69.007
Auckland 8

SOURCES OF INFORMATION

The Lace Guild
The Hollies
53 Audnam
Stourbridge
West Midlands DY8 4AE

The Lacemakers' Circle
49 Wardwick
Derby DE1 1HY

The Lace Society
Linwood
Stratford Road
Oversley
Alcester
War BY9 6PG

The British College of Lace
21 Hillmorton Road
Rugby
War CV22 5DF

The English Lace School
Oak House
Church Stile
Woodbury
Nr Exeter
Devon

International Old Lacers
President
Gunvor Jorgensen
366 Bradley Avenue
Northvale
NJ 076647 United States

United Kingdom Director of
  Internationa Old lacers
S. Hurst
4 Dollius Road
London N3 1RG

Ring of Tatters
Mrs C. Appleton
Nonesuch
5 Ryeland Road
Ellerby
Saltburn by Sea
Cleveland TS13 5LP

BOOKS

*The following are stockists of the complete
Batsford/Dryad Press range:*

Avon

Bridge Bookshop
7 Bridge Street
Bath BA2 4AS

Waterstone & Co.
4–5 Milsom Street
Bath BA1 1DA

Bedfordshire

Arthur Sells
Lane Cove
49 Pedley Lane
Clifton
Sefford SG17 5QT

Berkshire

West End Lace Supplies
Ravensworth Court Road
Mortimer West End
Reading RG7 3UD

Buckinghamshire

J. S. Sear Lacecraft Supplies
8 Hill View
Sherringham MK16 9NY

Cambridgeshire

Dillons the Bookstore
Sydney Street
Cambridge

Cheshire

Lyn Turner
Church Meadow Crafts
15 Carisbrook Drive
Winsford CW7 1LN

Devon

Creative Crafts & Needlework
18 High Street
Totnes TQ9 5NP

Honiton Lace Shop
44 High Street
Honiton EX14 8PJ

Dorset

F. Herring & Sons
High West Street
Dorchester DT1 1UP

Tim Parker (mail order)
124 Corhampton Road
Boscombe East
Bournemouth BH6 5NL

Durham

Lacemaid
6, 10 & 15 Stoneybeck
Bishop Middleham DL17 9BL

Gloucestershire

Southgate Handicrafts
68 Southgate Street
Gloucestershire GL1 1TX

Waterstone & Co.
89÷0 The Promenade
Cheltenham GL50 1NB

Hampshire

Creative Crafts
11 The Square
Winchester SO23 9ES

Doreen Gill
14 Barnfield Road
Petersfield GU31 4DR

Larkfield Crafts
4 Island Cottages
Mapledurwell
Basingstoke RG23 2LU

Needlestyle
24–26 West Street
Alresford

Ruskins
27 Bell Street
Romsey

Isle of Wight

Busy Bobbins
Unit 7
Scarrots Lane
Newport PO30 1JD

Kent

The Handicraft Shop
47 Northgate
Canterbury

Frances Iles
73 High Street
Rochester ME1 1LX

Lincolnshire

Rippingale Lace
Barn Farm House
off Station Road
Rippingdale Bourne

London

Foyles
119 Charing Cross Road WC2H 0EB

Hatchards
187 Piccadilly W1

Middlesex

Redburn Crafts
Squires Garden Centre
Halliford Road
Upper Halliford
Shepperton TW17 8RU

Norfolk

Alby Lace Museum
Cromer Road
Alby
nr Aylsham NR11 7QE

Jane's Pincushions
Taverham Craft Unit 4
Taverham Nursery Centre
Fir Covert Road
Taverham
Norwich NR8 6HT

Waterstone & Co.
30 London Street
Norwich NR2 1LD

Northamptonshire

D. J. Hornsby
149 High Street
Burton Latimer
Kettering NN15 5RL

Oxfordshire

Loricraft
19 Peregrine Way
Grove
Wantage

Scotland

Embroidery Shop
51 Withain Street
Edinburgh
Lothian EH3 7LW

Beverley Scarlett
Strupak
Hillhead
Coldwells
Ellon
Aberdeenshire

Waterstone & Co.
236 Union Street
Aberdeen AB1 1TN

Surrey

Needlestyle
5 The Woolmead
Farnham GU9 1TN

Sussex

Southern Handicrafts
20 Kensington Gardens
Brighton BN1 4AL

Warwickshire

Christine & David Springett
21 Hillmorton Road
Rugby CV22 6DF

North Yorkshire

Leeds LS28 9EB
Shireburn Lace
Finkel Court
Finkel Hill
Leeds LS25 6EA

Valley House Craft Studios
Ruston
Scarborough

West Midlands

Needlewoman
Needles Alley
off New Street
Birmingham

West Yorkshire

Sebalace
Waterloo Mill
Howden Road
Silsden BD20 0HA

George White Lacemaking Supplies
40 Heath Drive
Boston Spa LS23 6PB

Jo Firth
58 Kent Crescent
Lowtown
Pudsey

BIBLIOGRAPHY

EARNSHAW, PAT: *The Identification of Lace* (Shire Publications Ltd)
HEAD, MRS: *The Lace and Embroidery Collector: A Guide to Collectors of Old Lace and Embroidery* (Herbert Jenkins)
WARDLE, PATRICIA: *Victorian Lace* (Herbert Jenkins)

WRIGHT, THOMAS: *The Romance of the Lace Pillow – Being the History of Lace Making* (Paul P.B. Minet)
Needlecraft – Journal of Carrickmacross Lace (Manchester School of Embroidery)

INDEX